ARTIST TRANSCRIPTIONS PIANO

THE MASTERY OF Bill Evans

Piano Transcriptions and Performance Notes by Pascal Wetzel

T0083926

A close look at two classic compositions:
Waltz for Debby
Very Early

ISBN-13: 978-1-4234-1024-9
ISBN-10: 1-4234-1024-6

Folkways Music Publishers, Inc.

 The Richmond Organization

EXCLUSIVELY DISTRIBUTED BY

HAL•LEONARD®
CORPORATION
7777 W. BLUEMOUND RD. P.O. BOX 13819 MILWAUKEE, WI 53213

Visit Hal Leonard Online at
www.halleonard.com

Contents

Waltz for Debby

Very Early

WALTZ FOR DEBBY

"Waltz for Debby" (or "Waltze for Debby," since Evans used to spell 'waltz' with an e), was written during the summer of 1954, in honor of his older brother Harry's eldest daughter. "Very Early," another waltz, was written five years earlier.

"Waltz for Debby" was recorded for the first time in 1956 on *New Jazz Conceptions*, Evans' first album. It was played as a short piano solo without improvisation like a written classical composition–78 measures in the key of F. To illustrate the performance of the tune in this format, we present part of the arrangement written by Evans which appeared in the original edition of *Bill Evans Piano Solos*. Also included is a transcription of Evans' beautiful interpretation recorded on November 6, 1978 for the Marian McPartland's Piano Jazz National Public Radio program. In Bill's words, "this is more or less the original version" (except he added a short introduction).

A few years later, "Waltz for Debby" was recorded by a quartet with Cannonball Adderley. This was the first time that the piece was a vehicle for improvisation, changing to 4/4 time for a restatement of the theme and solos. With his own trio, Bill performed the tune this way most of the time (the Village Vanguard session of June 25, 1961 is a good example), but sometimes he stayed in 3/4 when improvising.

The third version of "Waltz for Debby" in this folio originally appeared in *Bill Evans 4* and is newly transcribed from *The Bill Evans Album*. When it was recorded in 1971, Evans had already recorded this tune several times, and decided that he wanted to do something different. He created a more elaborate trio arrangement: the theme is stated on solo acoustic piano freely in 3/4 in the key of A (one of his favorite keys), with a tag modulating to the original key of F by the use of chords descending by step, leading to a solo on electric piano in tempo with the rhythm section added. The time switches to 4/4 for a bass solo, another solo by Evans on acoustic piano, and the last theme with its famous short coda.

This classic composition is in the style of a show-tune. It is quite simple from a melodic and harmonic point of view: the progression of Section 1 is basically a 1 (III)-VI-II-V, cleverly enriched with bass lines, the use of substitute chords and secondary dominants, whereas the melodic rhythm is mainly dotted halves and quarter notes. But there are also superimposed rhythms (measures 63-70 of the written arrangement): a two-beat rhythm against the 3/4 meter, a device Evans used quite often in his compositions and improvisations.

"Waltz for Debby" is Evans' most famous tune. It remained in his repertoire till the end, and has been recorded by numerous instrumentalists both in and out of jazz. Thanks to Gene Lees' wonderful lyrics, the song has also been embraced by many singers as well.

WALTZ FOR DEBBY

BILL EVANS

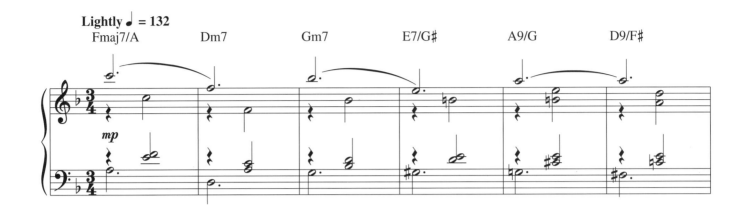

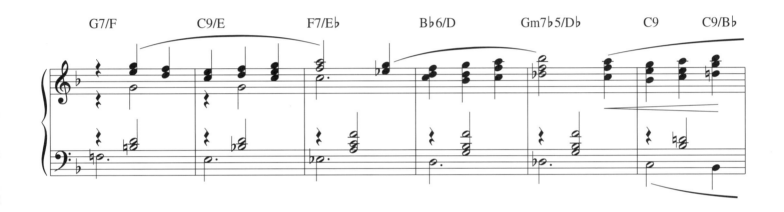

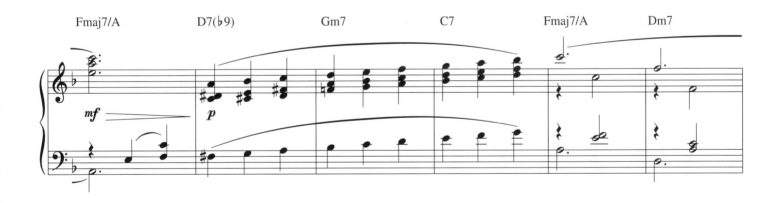

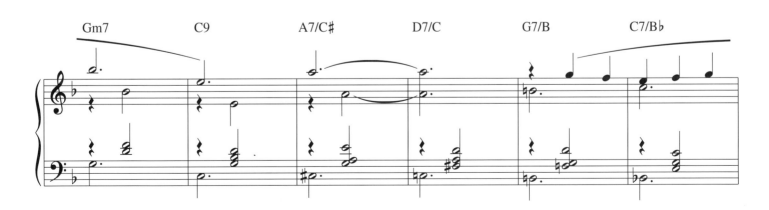

WALTZ FOR DEBBY
from "Marian McPartland's Piano Jazz Interview"

BILL EVANS

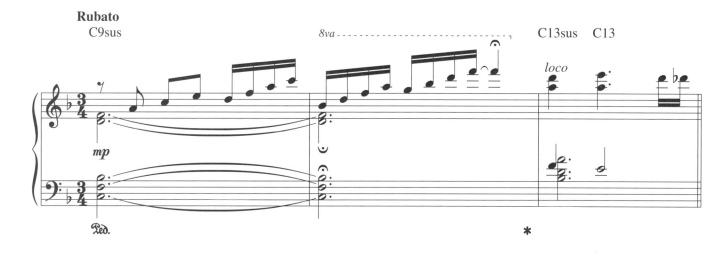

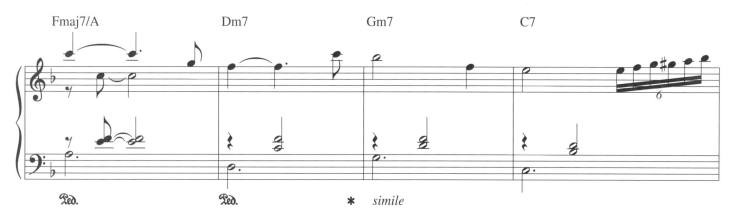

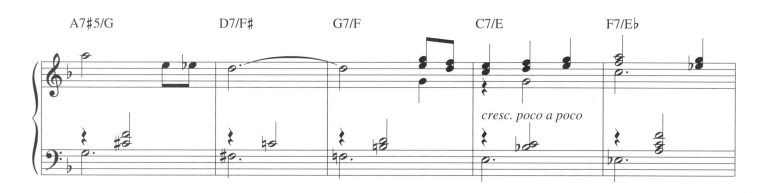

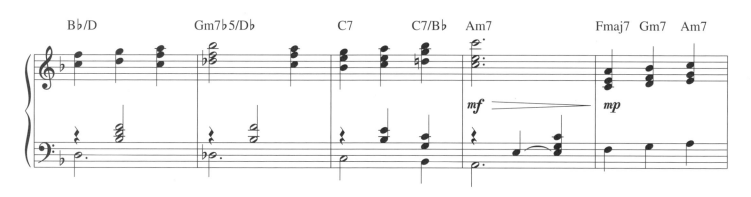

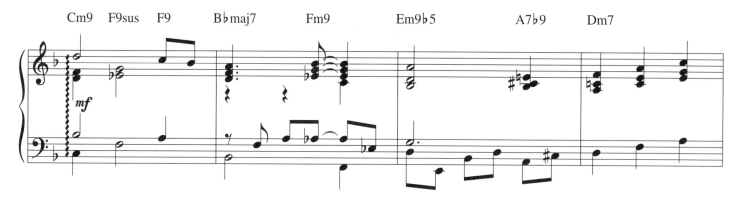

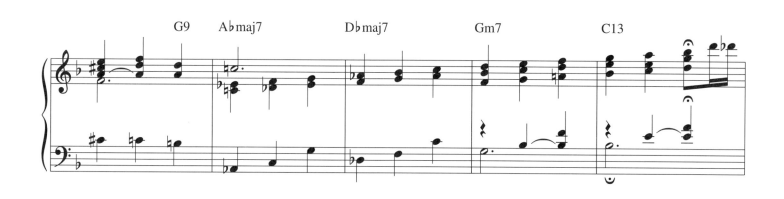

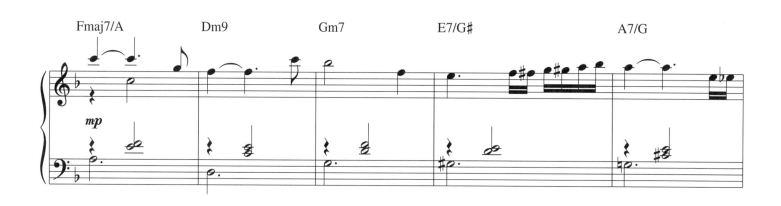

WALTZ FOR DEBBY

from *The Bill Evans Album*

BILL EVANS

Rubato (even 8ths)

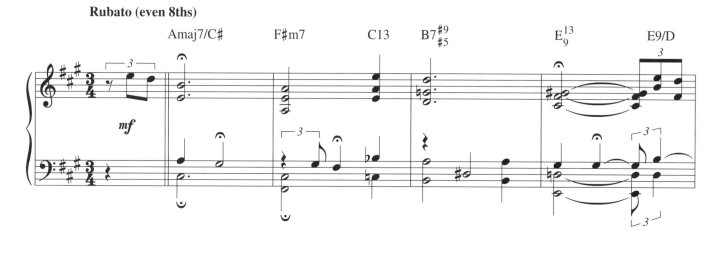

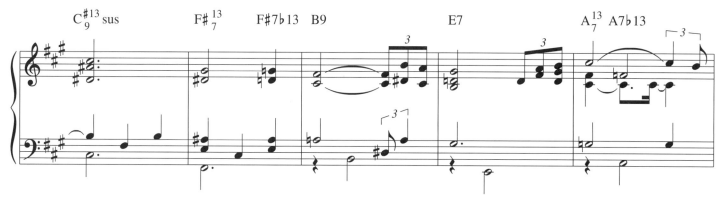

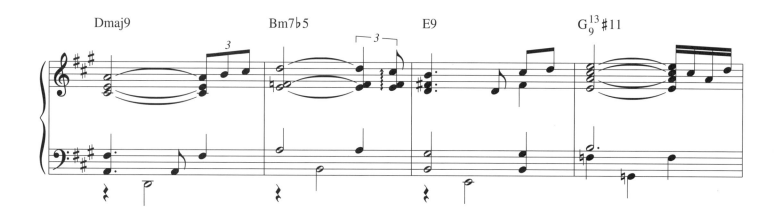

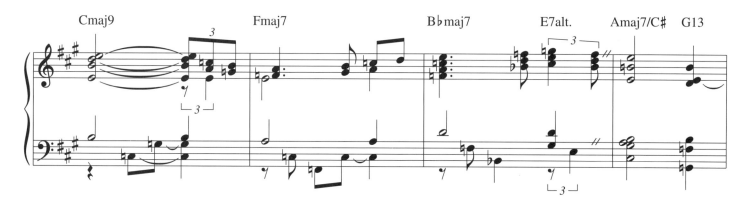

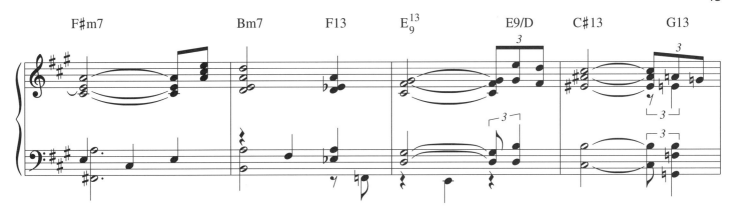

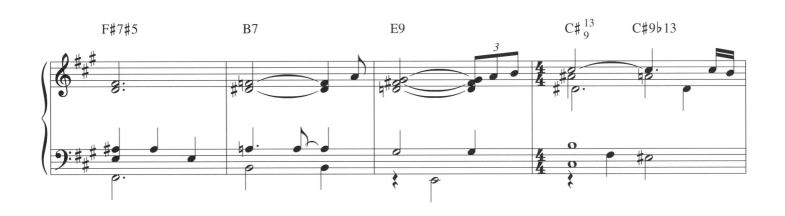

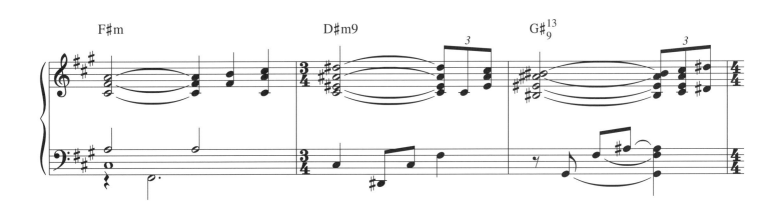

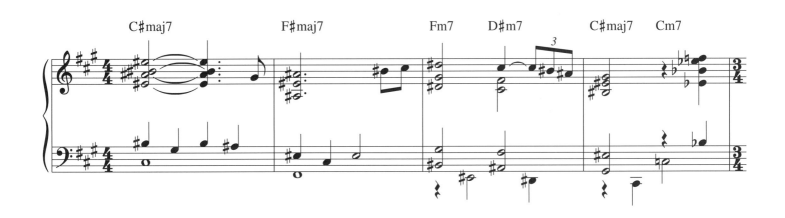

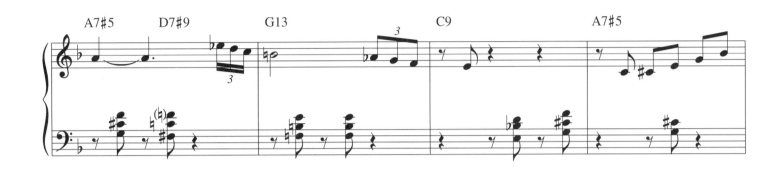

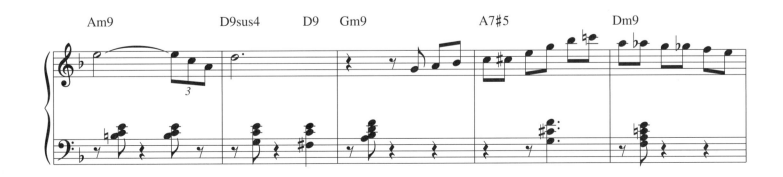

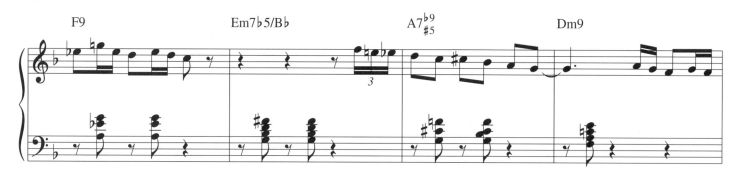

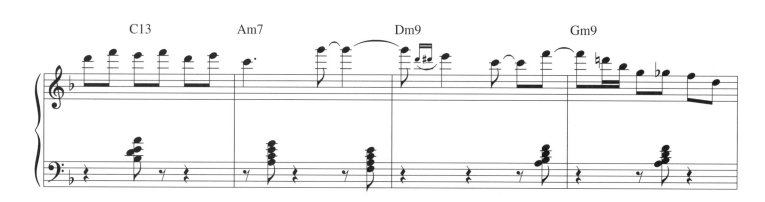

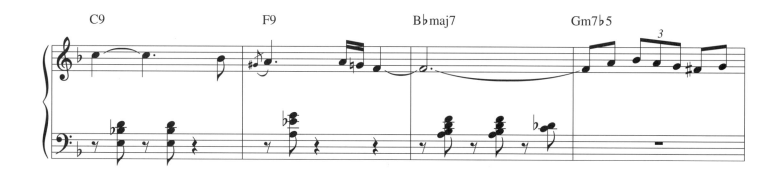

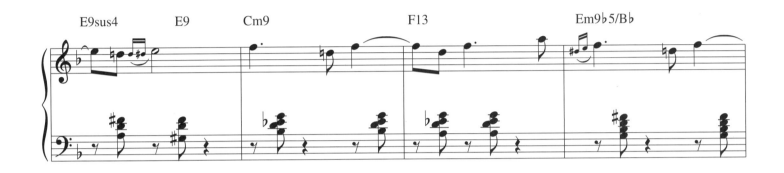

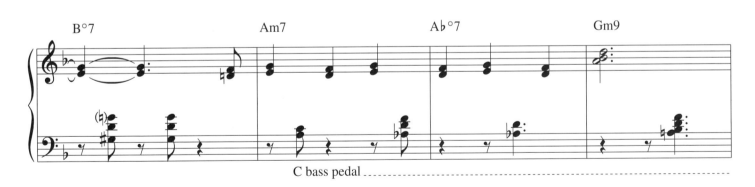

C bass pedal -

Bass Solo

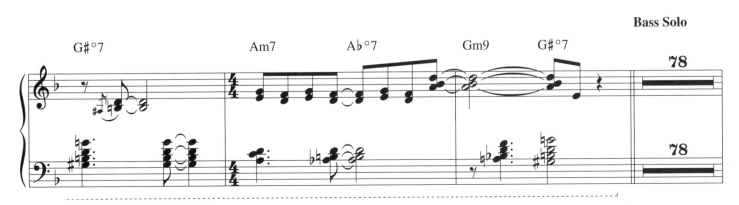

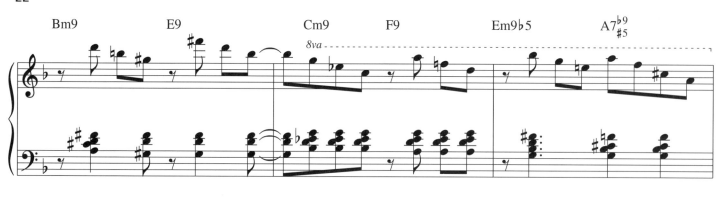

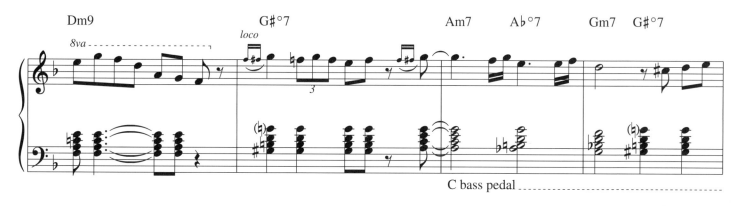

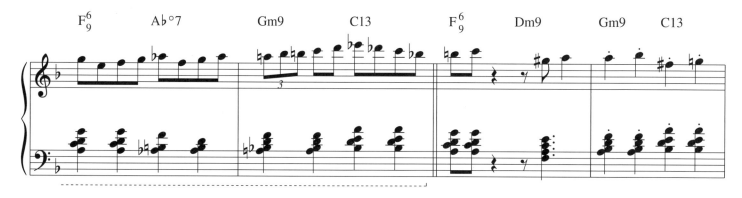

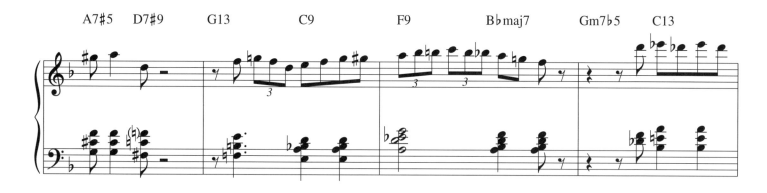

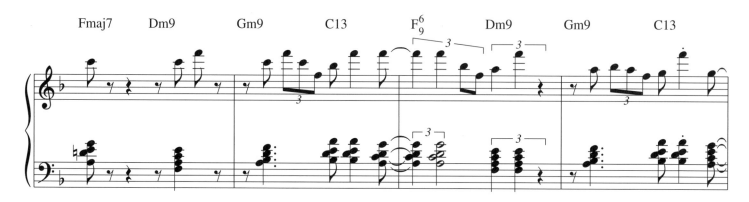

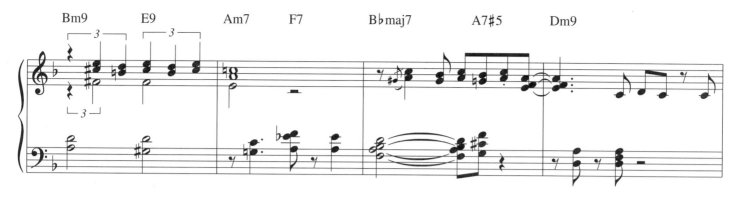

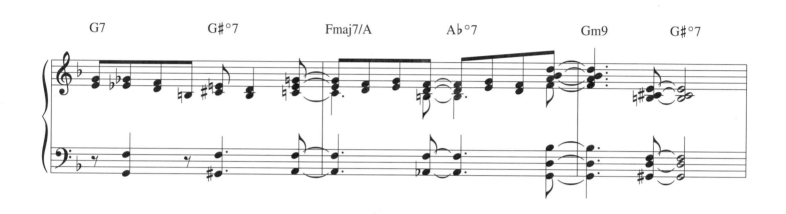

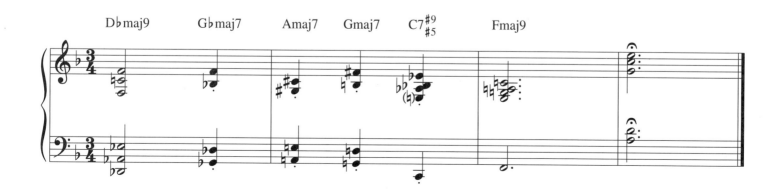

VERY EARLY

Bill Evans wrote "Very Early" as a composition assignment in 1948 or 1949 during his third year at Southeastern Louisiana College. He was nineteen years old. This masterpiece is the earliest composition that became part of his active repertoire, and the first of about a dozen compositions in 3/4 among the sixty-three original pieces published in the Evans fakebook. He obviously had an affinity for triple meter.

Two very different versions of "Very Early" are presented in this folio: the arrangement written by Evans for piano solo, and a transcription of a live performance by the trio on June 19, 1970 (appearing on the album *Montreux II*).

The first arrangement was written specifically for a printed folio; the piece was almost always performed by the trio. However, a solo version was filmed for the 1966 documentary *The Universal Mind of Bill Evans* (now available on DVD), where the right hand is simplified in the first section of the tune. A trio version recorded during March of 1966 (released as part of the boxed set *The Secret Sessions*) comes close to this arrangement.

The first studio recording of "Very Early" dates from 1962 for the album *Moonbeams*. It is surprising that Evans waited thirteen years to record the piece; seven other original compositions were recorded before this one. However, the tempo is moderate (♩ = 120-130), and it fits perfectly into this all-ballad album.

As time went on, the tempo noticeably increased, as shown in the Montreux version from 1970. Bill had not played for several weeks before this concert, but this is hard to believe when listening to his right-hand figures in his solo. The trio played a very swinging and dynamic version of what had been a gentle waltz, fired up by the enthusiastic audience in attendance. The tempo was slightly unsteady (Bill always had a strong tendency to push ahead, especially when performing in public) and the metronome markings speak for themselves: ♩ = 160, 184 and finally 194! In measures 24-26 of the second chorus, Bill started to play wrong chords (obviously borrowed by mistake from measures 40-42) before returning to the right changes.

"Very Early" is in AAB form divided into three groups of sixteen bars each. Evans obviously built the entire melodic frame in a logical way: two-bar motifs going down and up in a wide variety of intervals. Measures 41-44 show how he designed the melodic contour from two Major 7th chords a half-step apart:

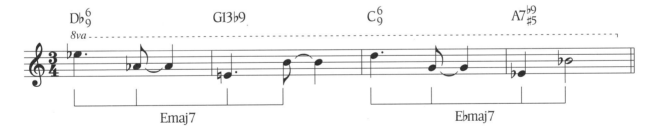

The B section is undoubtedly the peak of the tune. The melody is harmonized with right-hand triads in octaves for a full sound. The play-out tag is a classic with its rhythmic variations, the two-bar pattern played differently each time. This part of the composition remained unchanged, unlike the introduction: at Montreux as in Amsterdam (November 28, 1969, on the album *Quiet Now*), Evans abandoned the G Pedal he used to play for minor seventh chords moving upward by semitone to a II-V progression in C.

Unlike "Waltz for Debby," "Very Early" was always played in 3/4. With lyrics by Carol Hall, the song has also become popular with many jazz singers.

VERY EARLY

BILL EVANS

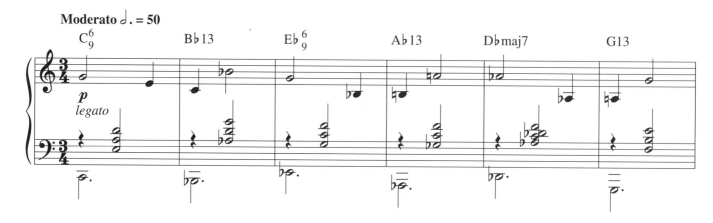

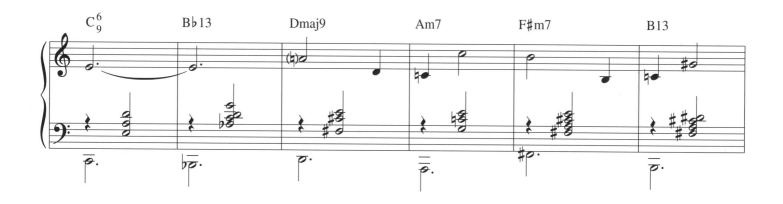

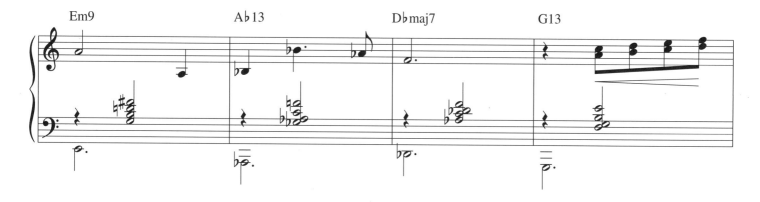

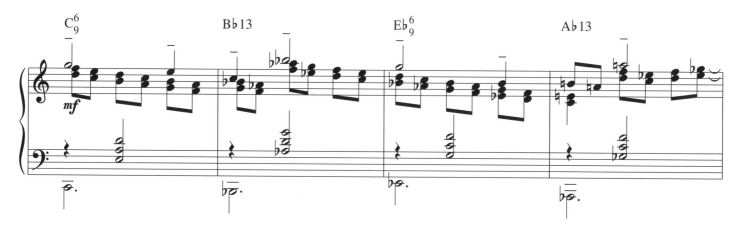

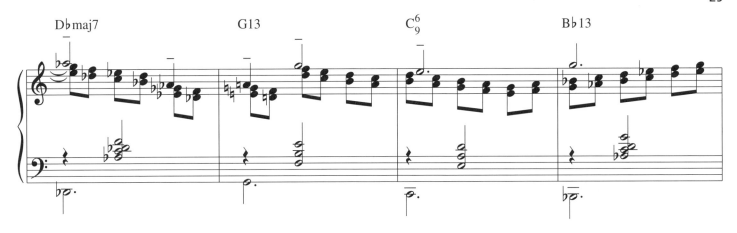

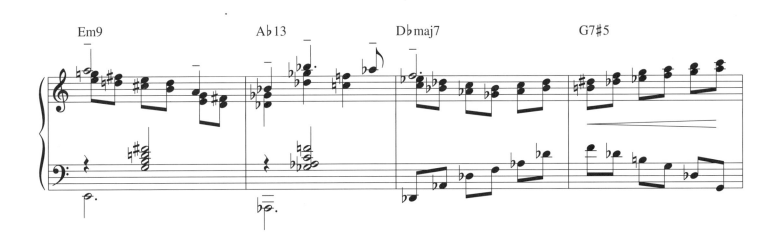

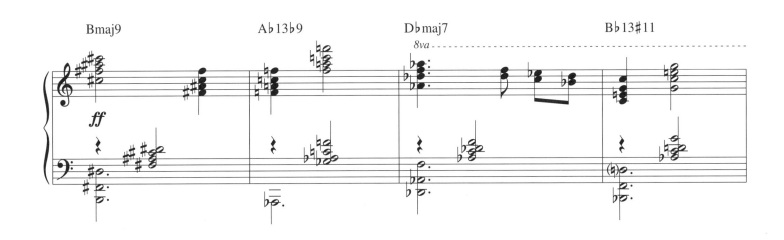

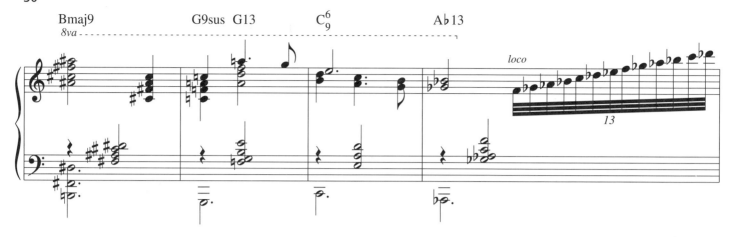

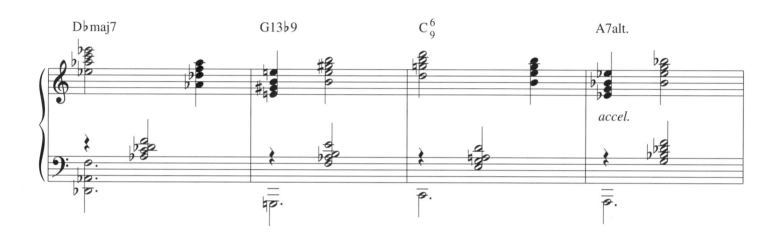

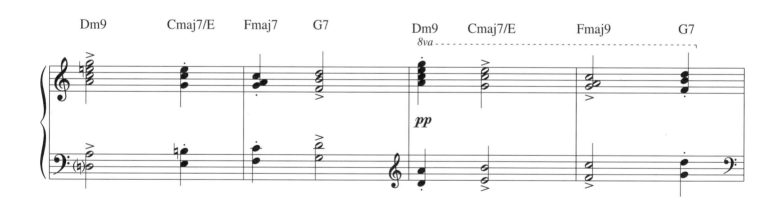

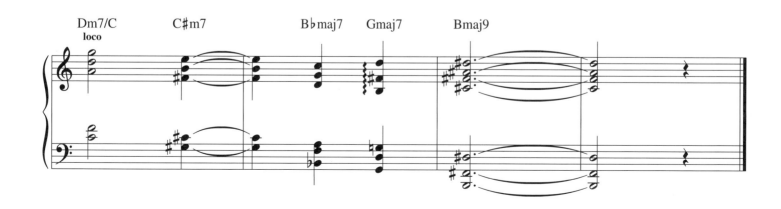

VERY EARLY
from *Montreux II*

BILL EVANS

Rubato

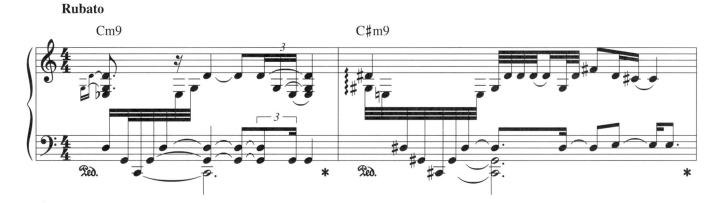

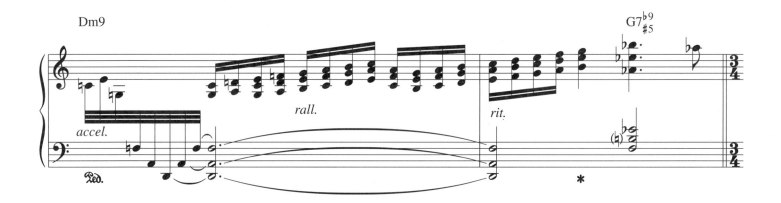

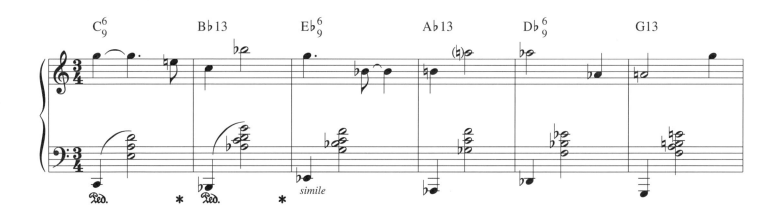

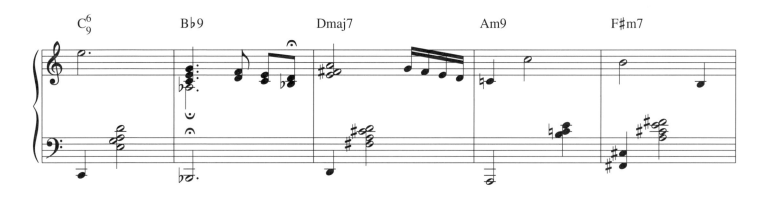

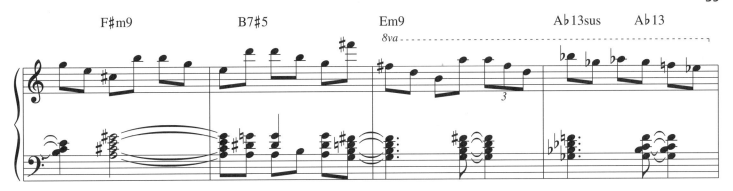

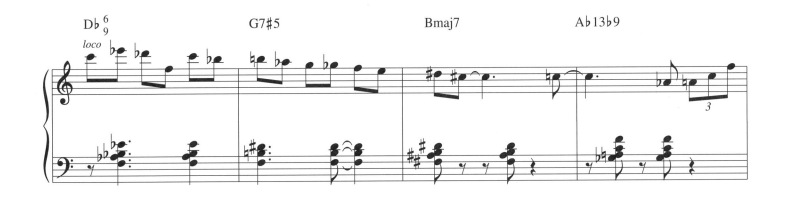

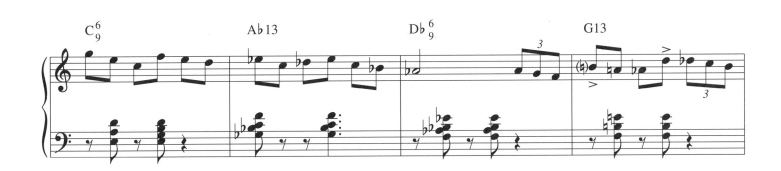

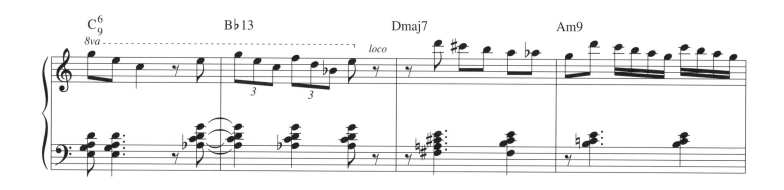

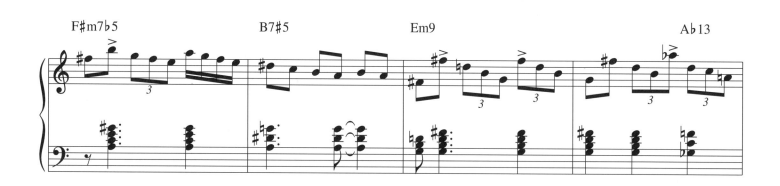

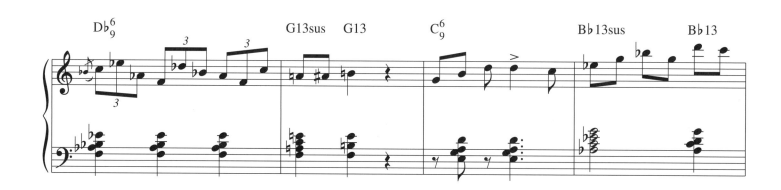

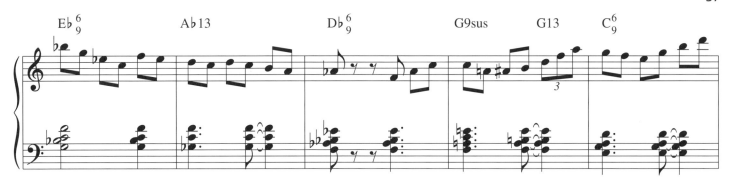

* Note that Bill Evans played wrong chords for 3 measures.

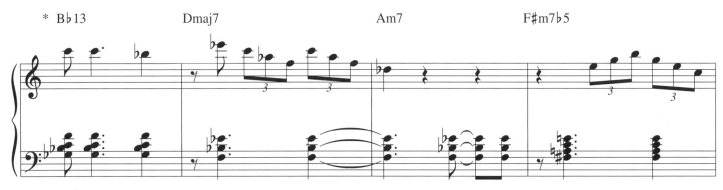

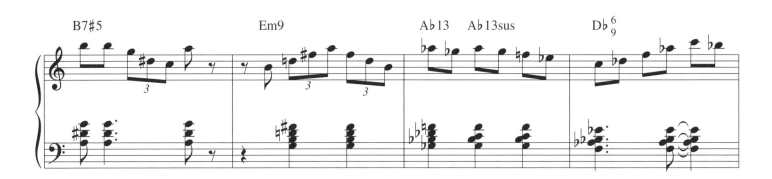

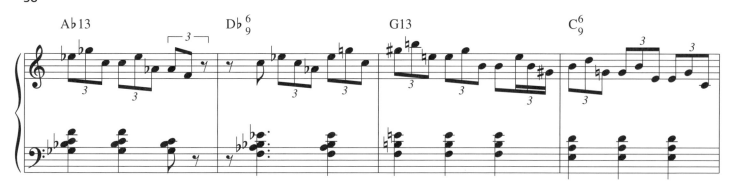

Bass Solo

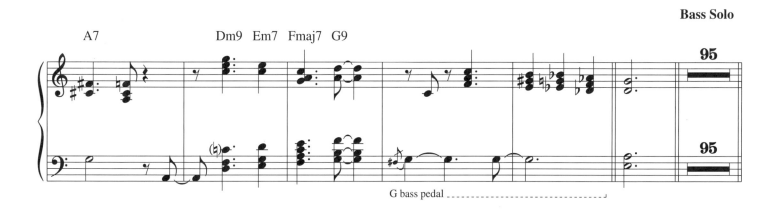

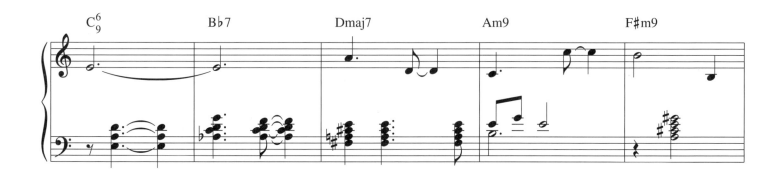

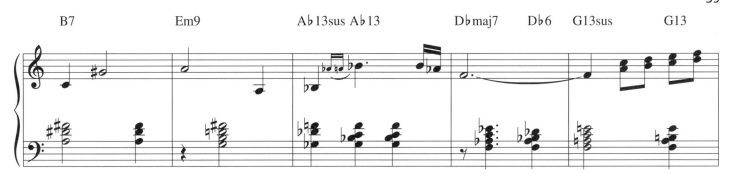

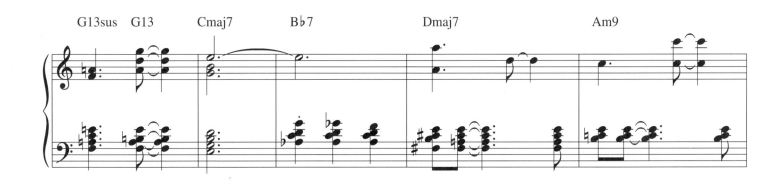

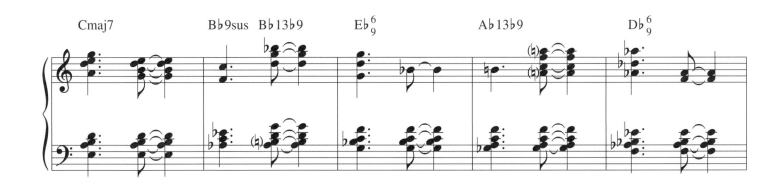

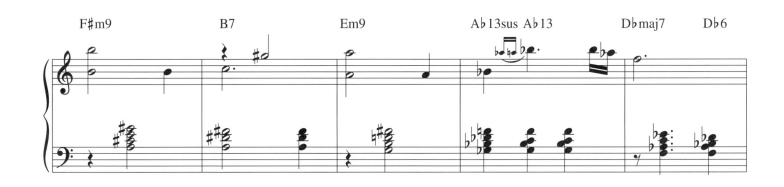

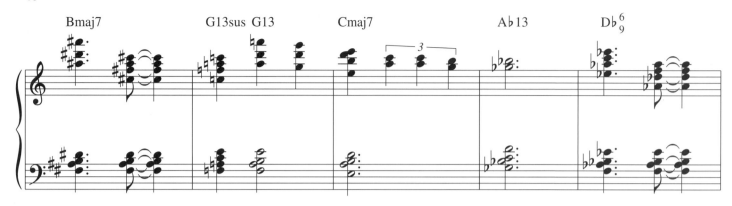

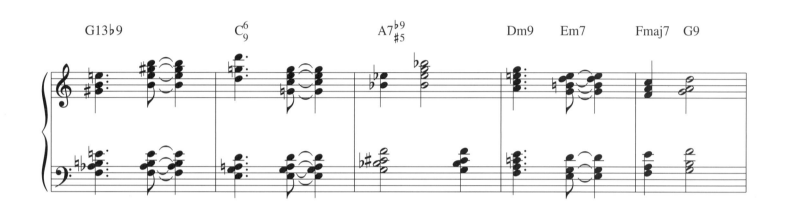

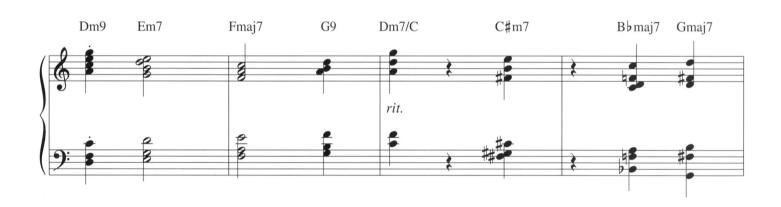